101 Liturgical Suggestions

Practical Ideas for Those who Prepare the Liturgy

Columba McCann

Published 2014 by
Veritas Publications
7–8 Lower Abbey Street
Dublin 1
Ireland
publications@veritas.ie
www.veritas.ie

ISBN 978 1 84730 553 4

10 9 8 7 6 5 4 3 2 1

A catalogue record for this book is available from the British Library.

Designed by Lir Mac Cárthaigh, Veritas
Printed in Ireland by Hudson Killeen Ltd, Dublin

Veritas books are printed on paper made from the wood pulp of managed forests. For every tree felled, at least one tree is planted, thereby renewing natural resources.

Contents

Introduction

This short book is not a systematic treatment of the theology or practice of liturgy. It is a series of practical suggestions, which come from working with liturgy preparation groups, meetings of liturgists and reflection on my own experience throughout the liturgical year. Parish liturgy groups are often enthusiastic about improving the celebrations of their local community, but at a loss as to where to begin. The suggestions in this book will present them with concrete ideas, while at the same time giving some instruction about basic liturgical principles. While the treatment is not systematic, the reader will, I hope, find that the suggestions are well informed by a broader reading of liturgical history and theological reflection. Many of the suggestions are also grouped into broad categories, for example: the turning of the year (nos. 3–35), the Mass (nos. 26–61), Baptism (nos. 62–66).

I would like to dedicate this short book to Fr Patrick Jones, who was my first teacher of liturgy back in the 1980s, and who continues the never-ending task of promoting good thinking and practice in this area. I probably first heard most of these ideas enunciated by him, either in class or at meetings, though I would not wish him to take the blame for any shortcomings in the pages that follow.

Start Small and Move Slowly

Faced with the need for liturgical renewal and the vast array of options, projects and undertakings that could be chosen, it is important to be modest and realistic in strategies for change. People often resist change, even when it is for the better. Changing ritual practices takes a lot of energy and much discussion is required in order to arrive at a consensus people can accept. If you want to renew your liturgy you are definitely 'in it for the long haul' and need to manage your resources. Make small improvements that have been discussed in advance and review them before going further.

Prepare Your Congregation for Any Changes You Are Planning

People can be confused, annoyed and downright resistant to changes which seem to appear out of nowhere without any apparent logic. Even a small adjustment to liturgical celebration becomes an opportunity to help people deepen their sense of what is involved in our liturgical gatherings. Prior notice and careful explanation, whether it be through preaching, parish newsletter, website or other means of communication, will help people to appreciate the effort that is being made for their benefit and will help them to engage well with proposed changes.

3

Until You Come Again

Our Sunday Eucharist is strewn with references to the Second Coming of Christ in glory, for example:

'You will come in glory with salvation for your people ...'
'He will come again in glory to judge the living and the dead ...'
'We proclaim your death, O Lord ... until you come in glory.'

This reflects a rediscovery in twentieth-century theology of the importance of eschatology. Despite this, it is rare that any discussion of the Second Coming makes its way into preaching, catechesis or other aspects of parish life. It is as if it simply doesn't fit in. The Second Coming often remains the preserve of the street preacher who, at least in caricature, preaches that 'the end of the world is nigh'.

Advent is an ideal time to consider this aspect of our faith and to allow it to trickle through our preaching, teaching and celebrating. Too often we fall into the trap of seeing Advent exclusively in terms of preparation for

Christmas. Yet a very deliberate decision was taken in the structuring of the present liturgical season. References to Christmas and its preparation are relatively mute until 17 December. Early Advent has the focus more clearly on the Second Coming.

Let's not be afraid to give references to the Second Coming a proper place in our Advent liturgies. We live in a time when people are anxious about the future of planet earth. Advent provides us with a bright vision of the future that God has in mind for our world. It can become an encouragement to live this vision even now.

4

Let the Advent Wreath Speak for Itself

Part of the power of symbols lies in their ambiguity: they question, puzzle and invite reflection and imagination. They speak at various levels and their effect is not simply on the level of intellectual understanding. Trying to explain symbols reduces their meaning; it flattens them into mere teaching aids. If there is to be an Advent wreath this year, let's drop the explanations. There is nothing wrong with being puzzled!

Notice Mary, the Mother of God, as a Special Model of Discipleship During Advent

Although centred on the person of Christ, Advent is also, in a certain sense, a natural season of Mary. She is the model disciple. The coming to birth within her of Christ, through obedience to God's word and the power of the Holy Spirit, is the story also of what must happen in us. Perhaps these weeks are a time for some additional decoration at the Marian shrine in your church building.

An Advent Carol Service

One of the concerns of the Second Vatican Council was the relationship between liturgical rites and the culture of those who celebrate. It was realised that a 'one size fits all' approach was not the best. People should be able to celebrate in a ritual language that is true to the Christian tradition and yet their own at the same time. The task of grafting new cultures onto our tradition and making the appropriate adaptations is not easy. Not everything in a local culture fits well within the Christian vision. Sometimes we have to be counter-cultural. The season of Advent is a case in point.

The season of Advent does not exist in the commercial world. Christmas songs begin playing in the shops as soon as Halloween is over. This is not to decry the activities of shopkeepers; they have to make a living. With Christmas shopping, Christmas parties and other such activities in full swing by early December, the 'Christmas season' for many people ends on Christmas Day. Within the liturgical year it only begins on 25 December.

An Advent service is one antidote that can help people regain a better sense of focus. Readings, prayers and songs can strike a chord within the heart, opening up that deep longing for God's presence and deepening our sense of hope amid the difficulties of life. The temptation can be to have a service of Christmas carols, thus dropping the Advent flavour altogether. This can be a real difficulty for some groups, such as schools and colleges, where people are not together for Christmas itself. The desire to celebrate Christmas before the end of term in these situations tends to push Advent off the map. A compromise is to ensure that there is a fair amount of Advent material in the service, Christmas carols notwithstanding. The first half of the service can have Advent readings, prayers and songs. If the service is well received by those who attend, perhaps the Advent content could be increased slightly each year, as people become more comfortable with this way of celebrating.

Develop Some Traditions for an Advent Service

Advent so easily gets swallowed up in the pre-Christmas rush. In some places an effort is made to rehabilitate this season by having an Advent service, perhaps on the afternoon of the First Sunday of Advent. One does not have to reinvent the wheel when it comes to planning it; the readings of the four Sundays of Advent could provide a possible structure. The responsorial psalms of these days, along with Advent hymns, gospel acclamations and sung intercessions can supply a musical dimension.

The darkness of winter opens up the possibility of doing something visual with lighted candles – perhaps connected with the Advent wreath. The use of incense for the main gospel reading will add another dimension. Some testimony from lay parishioners about what Advent means to them might be a welcome alternative to a homily. Include some familiar prayers and songs, so that people do not feel 'at sea'. The Our Father is an obvious prayer to use towards the end. A solemn blessing and a blessing of Christmas food might conclude. The service need not be long, but it could be memorable.

'Change Key' on 17 December

The mood of the readings and liturgy of Advent changes from 17 December on. Something of the joyful antici-pation of Christmas creeps into the liturgy. On the Advent wreath this is symbolised by the rose-coloured candle. Perhaps this could also be reflected in the general way in which the church is decorated for this season – the colour of the flowers, for example. On the other hand, it is important to keep those elements which are proper to Christmas itself (for example, the crib and the singing of Christmas carols) until Christmas actually arrives.

Bless the Christmas Tree and Put it in the Right Place

It seems at times that Christmas has been taken over by Tinseltown. The twinkle of fairy lights in our streets may be more about encouraging spending than anything else. And yet fundamental symbols are being used, which are not at all incompatible with the liturgy. The cross is the tree of life. Christ is the light of the world. The Book of Blessings includes a blessing of a Christmas tree for use inside the church building. We should take care, however, that the Christmas tree, Advent wreath or even the Christmas crib itself do not detract from the fundamental liturgical symbols: bread, wine, altar, ambo, baptismal font and so on. When it comes to decorating our churches at Christmastime, it is best to use the whole church building, rather than cluttering everything into the sanctuary area.

Celebrate the Glory of Christ Today at Christmas

When it comes to looking at the readings of the Christmas season, a particularly influential book in recent times has been *An Adult Christ at Christmas* by the late Raymond Brown. One should never judge a book by its cover, and perhaps not even by its title, but this particular title should alert us to stop and think about our pastoral approach to the Christmas season. We know that the gospels were written not just to record some key events and teachings from the earthly life of Jesus but also, and perhaps more importantly, to help Christian communities to recognise the presence of the risen Christ among them and to respond to his call. Scripture is about a living reality among us now and so is liturgy, which flows from hearing God's word. It is important then that our preaching, our singing, our church decorations and all the different aspects of our celebration of Christmas should open us up to the risen Christ. The Christmas crib, for all its beauty, its pathos and its eloquence about the humility and simplicity of God's approach, can degenerate into a sentimental 'storybook' image of a highly romanticised past event. Let's make sure that it becomes a sign of the God who today in Christ comes among us according to our human flesh. The infancy narratives of the gospels speak in miniature of the whole mystery of Christ among us, active, crucified, risen. Our Christmas celebrations should do the same.

New Year's Resolutions

Here are twelve liturgical New Year's resolutions. You might like to choose one or two of them or, alternatively, you could implement one of them each month.

- At the principal Mass on Sunday, we will ensure that the response to the psalm is sung.
- At every Mass the gospel acclamation will be either sung or omitted.
- Readings will be proclaimed from the lectionary and not from flimsy missalettes.
- The ambo will be reserved for proclaiming, preaching and praying the scriptural word of God. It will not be used for announcements or other activities.
- At Sunday Masses the intentions of the Prayer of the Faithful will be read by a parish reader.
- At all Masses the bread and wine to be consecrated will be brought forward by members of the congregation and presented to the priest.
- At all Masses people will receive the Eucharist that has been consecrated at the same Mass. Recourse to the tabernacle will be by way of exception.

- Communion under both kinds will become a normal activity in the parish.
- On special occasions throughout the year we will introduce people to attractive celebrations of the Liturgy of the Hours. This will be the beginning of a longer process towards making this a more frequent liturgical celebration, which can be arranged in the absence of an ordained priest.
- We will review the physical arrangements in our church building in relation to people with disabilities.
- At funerals we will arrange for a suitable location for mementos of the deceased instead of receiving them as 'offertory gifts'. They will be put in place either before the funeral Mass or at the reception of the body.
- We will devote considerable energy to the training and ongoing formation of parish readers, since the life of the parish as a Christian community depends on our hearing the word of God.

Celebrate the Baptism of the Lord, and Ours Too

The Feast of the Baptism of the Lord not only recalls the Baptism of Jesus but also celebrates our identification with him through our own Baptism. An obvious way to highlight this aspect of the celebration is to have the blessing and sprinkling of water at the beginning of Mass. This is an attractive alternative to the penitential rite, and is underused in many parishes. It is important that the sprinkling itself be accompanied by an appropriate song. On a really festive occasion the rite can be amplified by involving a number of people in the bringing forward of the water and its being poured into a vessel for blessing.

This day may also be a suitable occasion for some publicity about preparation for Baptism: give people a general outline of the pre-baptismal work that is done with parents and the general thinking behind it. The Baptism of adults is an increasing phenomenon, and some reflection on the RCIA (Rite of Christian Initiation of Adults) will become more and more necessary in every parish.

Give Some Catechesis on the Meaning of Holy Water

The Feast of the Baptism of the Lord might be a good occasion for catechesis on the meaning and use of holy water. Many people are unaware that holy water serves as a reminder of Baptism. This is expressed in the words used to introduce the blessing and sprinkling of water at Mass. If water is blessed and sprinkled on this day, perhaps people could be encouraged to take some home with them and to use it in memory of their own Baptism.

Present Your Congregation with a Variety of Spiritual Practices in Advance of Lent

Before Lent it would be a good idea to present people with a number of concrete ideas for how they might live this season. Daily Mass is a popular option but there are other liturgical and spiritual resources to be introduced to people: Liturgy of the Hours, *lectio divina*, Third World aid, sponsored fasts, Stations of the Cross, rosary, pilgrimage, to name a few. As Lent is a special time for those preparing for Christian initiation, a special focus could be on prayer and accompaniment of those preparing for Baptism, Confirmation or First Holy Communion. Another element worth focusing on during Year C of the Sunday Lectionary is the Sacrament of Reconciliation, as there is a particular focus in this year on sin and forgiveness on the third, fourth and fifth Sundays of Lent. Perhaps on the weekend before Ash Wednesday there could be a gathering at which some of these possibilities could be presented. The gathering could include a festive Shrove Tuesday element and could finish up with the lighting of a bonfire in which the ashes for the following Wednesday are prepared.

Cultivate Lent as a Time of Sacramental Preparation

Late summer/early autumn is presumably the time of year for planning the ongoing initiation of children who have already been baptised. It would be a good thing to try to harmonise the timing of these sacraments and their preparation with the rhythm of the liturgical year. Lent is a time of more intense preparation for the sacraments of initiation and a time of penance. At the beginning of Lent those preparing for Confirmation and First Holy Communion might make some commitment suitable to their age to prepare during Lent. They will need support and help from people, such as parents, faith friends and teachers. A small number of those confirmed in recent years might also be willing to be involved. The candidates could also be prayed for each Sunday during the Prayer of the Faithful. This approach will give a stronger focus and meaning to Lent for them. The Sacrament of Penance could be celebrated for the first time towards the end of Lent. The Easter season then becomes the ideal time for Confirmation and First Holy Communion.

Introduce the Possibility of Variety During Your Lenten Observance

Lent is not a season of willpower. Nor it is it a test to see how strong we are. Keeping a particular Lenten resolution right to the bitter end is not the goal. Lent is a season in which the Holy Spirit searches our hearts and uncovers our wounds and weaknesses, bringing healing and strength. People sometimes give up after a week or so because they have not lived up to the task they have set themselves. Each week, new ideas based on the readings of the Sunday could be suggested either in the homily, notices or bulletin. A Lenten practice can be for all forty days, for a week or even for a single day.

Prepare for Palm Sunday

The beginning of Lent is a good time to start thinking about Holy Week and how its liturgy could be improved. Palm Sunday is a case in point. The blessing of palms and procession are often rather minimalistic in our celebrations. It would be good, for example, to use real branches for at least some of the participants, and not just hand-sized twigs. If candles are to be carried, get candlesticks with protective coverings so that the flame is not blown out. When it comes to the proclamation of the Passion on this day, try to refrain from using the altar as a reading stand just because it happens to have a microphone; keep the altar for the Liturgy of the Eucharist. There is nothing to stop two or even three readers using the ambo together, unless of course its design prevents this. Thought might be given in the long run to having an ambo large enough to take more than one reader at a time.

Name the Three Days of the Easter Triduum

The days of the Sacred Triduum are Good Friday, Holy Saturday and Easter Sunday, celebrating Christ crucified, buried and risen. The liturgy of Holy Thursday is a kind of overture which, recalling the institution of the Eucharist and the washing of feet, sums up the meaning of all that is to take place. It is a good idea when putting together church notices and calendars to try to reflect the true significance of each day of the Triduum. The Easter Vigil should also be late enough at night to be a real beginning of Easter Sunday.

The Good Friday Prayers are Long, so Use the Changes of Posture Suggested in the Missal to Keep the Mind and Heart Focused

The general intercessions on Good Friday are a solemn and lengthy part of this liturgy. The Missal directs that they be said with the people either kneeling throughout, standing throughout, or standing for the invitations to prayer and kneeling for the prayers themselves. Most liturgical planners opt for a uniform posture because it is easier. A continual change of posture does however provide more variety. Movement of the body also focuses the prayer and concentrates the mind. For those who are able, a change of posture at each prayer may in fact be spiritually preferable.

Celebrate a People-Friendly Form of Morning Prayer on Holy Saturday

Many parishes in Ireland have a sizeable and consistent daily Mass congregation. During Lent and into Holy Week, the numbers often grow. Holy Saturday morning is a time when there is no Mass, yet many people would like to have some form of liturgical prayer on this morning. An obvious possibility is some simple form of Liturgy of the Hours. A visual focus for the celebration could be the pieta, the cross or a representation of the tomb. Perhaps a devotional addendum could be for people to bring forward flowers at the end of the celebration and lay them around this visual symbol of the death of Christ. Later they can be taken up and used to provide some of the lavish decoration of the Easter Vigil.

Spend Some Weeks Designing the Kind of Font in which Water will be Blessed During the Easter Vigil

Lent is the time to start some advanced planning for the Easter Vigil. One important aspect is the baptismal liturgy, whether it be the celebration of Baptism itself or the renewal of baptismal promises. In either case, thought could be given to the vessel in which the baptismal water is blessed. Try to envisage something really beautiful and attractive. Think of the whole ensemble of vessel, place of display, floral or other decoration, light, etc. Some parishes have gone as far as to purchase the kind of container that underlies a garden fountain and have built up something really impressive. This may, in fact, turn out to be a far more powerful symbol than the attempt to recreate the empty tomb in an Easter garden; the font reaches back to the death and resurrection of Christ, connects us to our own Baptism and invites us here and now to renew this connection in a bodily way, while the staging of a tomb (good though it may be) works through the more superficial dynamic of make-believe.

Use Water During the Easter Season

A message which is coming through with increasing clarity from parishes around the country is that our liturgies are weighed down with words, and at the same time symbolically impoverished. Actions can speak louder than words. In the season of Easter, the sprinkling of water at the beginning of Mass each Sunday is a very appropriate way of continuing the baptismal image of the Easter Vigil. If you are going to sprinkle water, use plenty of it. A few drops sprinkled in the general direction of the congregation won't speak much of new life, growth or the Holy Spirit. Ideally the sprinkling is accompanied by singing. A simple refrain that everyone can join in would be enough.

Simple gestures like this will help to keep alive a sense of the ongoing celebration of Easter. These Sundays are, after all, not Sundays after Easter but Sundays of Easter.

Consider the Use of Various Languages at the Feast of Pentecost

The celebration of the outpouring of the Holy Spirit at Pentecost is marked by an awareness of the worldwide missionary dynamic of the gospel. The word of God was proclaimed in many languages at Pentecost and has taken root in many nations. Such a day might be an opportunity to celebrate the diversity of background in some of our congregations. One might consider a greater variety of language during the liturgy; for example, in the songs (where some music from Taizé might be very appropriate), in the intercessions and in the homily.

Work Hard on Improving the Celebration of Ordinary Time

During Ordinary Time the opportunity arises to look at our 'ordinary' celebrations. Hopefully Christmas, Easter and the other 'strong seasons' will have known some memorable moments of celebration. It is tempting however for liturgical planners to concentrate on special feasts and seasons. A far more demanding task is to try to gradually improve the quality of celebration on the 'ordinary' Sunday or weekday. Perhaps a good way to start would be to work through the General Instruction of the Roman Missal as a structure for reflecting on current practice and how it could be improved. A useful and very practical publication was produced by the National Centre for Liturgy in 2005, *Celebrating the Mystery of Faith: A Guide to the Mass*. The slow, patient work of examining our celebrations, looking for better options and gradually introducing appropriate adjustments could form an agenda for a number of years.

Make Solemnities More Festive than Feasts, and Feasts more Festive than Memorias

Some solemnities, like Christmas and Easter, are already truly festive in every way. Others, especially when they fall on a weekday, can seem anything but festive or celebrative in style. One does of course have to be realistic about the resources available for some weekday celebrations. Perhaps a little more singing could be added on solemn occasions. The creative use of church bells could also be considered. But perhaps the simplest and most effective way to signal the relative importance of a particular day is through the visual medium. One could, for example, have two altar candles lit for ordinary days and memorias, four for feasts, and six for solemnities. The lighting of additional candles or lamps around the church can also be reserved for solemnities.

The manner in which the altar is dressed could vary according to the degree of solemnity. More festive vestments could be kept for the more special occasions. With so many images available to us nowadays it is also possible to reflect the importance of a particular day with beautiful illustrations combined with some background information on the church notice board.

Help People to Sing

Irish congregations do sing, but sometimes, through lack of encouragement, persistence and proper planning, they don't. The following tips may help liturgical planners who wish to improve congregational singing:

- People sing short refrains much more easily than long verses.
- Some music will need to be repeated from week to week if the congregation is to grow accustomed to singing.
- The more important chants of the Mass have popular settings which in fact use refrains, for example: the Gospel Acclamation, the Memorial Acclamation, the Great Amen, the Responsorial Psalm. It is wise to begin working on congregational singing by focusing on just one or two of these for a few weeks. As the texts are well known, hymnals or sheets are not normally necessary.
- Pick very easy settings to start.
- A minimum number of pieces should be repeated for a month, a season or even a whole year.

- It is quite permissible, for the sake of congregational singing, to use the same responsorial psalm over a period of weeks. Obviously the psalm will need to be carefully chosen if this approach is adopted.
- People will be more inclined to sing if there is a cantor who is able to rehearse one or two pieces with them briefly before Mass and who can continue to encourage them to sing during the celebration itself. This person need not be a magnificent singer but must be a good encourager.
- If a leaflet is being used, those parts which are to be sung by everyone should be clearly marked. When the word 'choir' appears after a title the congregation are less likely to join in. Words such as 'all sing' are helpful before the appropriate refrains.
- If people do not know the words of a particular piece off by heart, it is not fair to them to expect them to sing unless a text is provided for them.
- The entrance song should normally be one in which everyone can join with ease, otherwise a passive tone will be set for all the remaining music of the liturgy.
- The use of congregational-friendly music at certain key points in the Mass need not prevent a parish choir preparing more elaborate pieces which they

sing on their own, especially for the Preparation of Gifts and Holy Communion.

- 'They won't sing' can often be a self-fulfilling prophecy: we don't really believe they will sing, so we won't really bother providing them with the help they need and so they don't actually sing!

- It takes a long time to educate a passive congregation into active participation, and most musicians give up far too early. The first few weeks may be difficult, it may even take a year or two, or longer, before real progress is made. Be patient and persevere.

Be Hospitable

'Let all guests who arrive be received like Christ, for he is going to say, "I came as a guest, and you received me."'

These words from the *Rule of St Benedict* emphasise the importance of Christian hospitality. Hospitality is not, of course, something just for monks, but should be the special care of every Christian. Our own hearts can be deeply touched when someone makes the extra effort to welcome us as visitors. A house that truly welcomes is a very special place indeed. If hospitality is one of the hallmarks of our daily living, it should be even more a feature of our liturgical celebrations. Fundamental questions for liturgical planners could be: How welcoming is our church building? Does it invite people to come in and remain? Does it cater for those who have hearing difficulties? Or for those who use wheelchairs? Is it warm? When the Prodigal Son arrived home a ring was put on his finger, sandals on his feet, and the best of food was laid on. Does our liturgical celebration speak the same message? Is our church furnished in the same spirit? In our use of bread, wine, water, oil, candles, flowers and music do we have an approach that is generous, wholesome and true? Or do we go for the minimum and even the artificial?

Hospitality is also about how we are with one another. The Irish *teach an phobail* (house of the people) indicates that the church building belongs to us all and that what is really needed is a sense of mutual welcome. It seems strange that we can go through the whole of Mass, up to the Sign of Peace, before acknowledging the people around us. A compromise that may help generate a broader sense of welcome is to develop a ministry of hospitality. This means designating people who take care of those who enter the building: giving them a leaflet if necessary, helping them to their seats as appropriate, and generally turning what can be a cold, anonymous experience into something more human.

When the two disciples along the road welcomed the stranger, listening to him and inviting him to stay for supper, they discovered that they were in the presence of the risen Lord. If we wish to deepen our appreciation of the Lord's eucharistic presence, a greater commitment to hospitality may be an important key.

Use the Colours of the Liturgical Seasons

Altar cloths are traditionally white. It is however possible to introduce the colours of the liturgical seasons and feasts: violet for Advent and Lent, red for Pentecost, etc. A simple solution is to have a coloured cloth which reaches down to the ground on either side of the altar. A white cloth which simply covers the altar table itself can be placed on top. Not every altar is designed to take a cloth which reaches to the ground in the manner described, so some care is needed in coming to a decision.

Make Music a Normal Part of Every Mass

Music plays a vital role in the liturgy. In the new General Instruction of the Roman Missal, it is presumed that singing of some form will take place in every Mass. Sometimes it may simply be an Alleluia acclamation before the gospel, a memorial acclamation and the great amen and the end of the Eucharistic Prayer. No great expertise is required to do this, simply someone who is willing to start the singing at the appropriate moments.

The possibility of some instrumental music need not be overlooked. There is a shortage of organists in many parishes, and perhaps thought should be given to investing some money in training piano players so that they will gain some proficiency at the organ as well. Every parish has someone who can play. Traditional musicians also abound and yet, strangely, are rarely heard in church. A slow air can be a haunting accompaniment to the Preparation of Gifts or the procession to Communion.

Connect Your Parish Musicians with Those in Other Parishes

The ministry of music is demanding and sometimes participants are in need of support and refreshment. One possible avenue is to organise occasional meetings of choirs and choir directors in a local area. For example, singers in a cluster of parishes could come together with their leaders and share with one another the music they are learning for a particular liturgical season. In this way, their repertoire is enriched, they experience the support and the variety of singing with other music groups and the music ministry is given fresh impetus. The feelgood factor works hand in hand with the possibility of a wider vision of how to take on the challenges of providing good music.

Make Sure That Ministers Communicate Before Mass Begins

Many practical problems in liturgical celebrations boil down to a lack of good communication: the reader didn't know which reading to read, the priest didn't know the Gloria was going to be sung, the Eucharistic Minister didn't realise that Communion was being brought to the sick from Mass. One could compile a much longer list of such instances. A very simple solution is to have a policy that all ministers, including the music director, should call into the sacristy before Mass.

Vary the Introduction at the Beginning of Mass

The Missal gives a text for the introduction to the Mass, but many presiders prefer to put something of their own together to suit each occasion. For those who wish to do this, the following pointers may be helpful:

- Some presiders use this moment as an opportunity to introduce some of the themes of the readings. Remember, however, that an introduction may be given directly before each reading. The latter approach may be more useful, given the average attention span of most listeners.
- Another approach is to take a theme or image from the opening prayer of the Mass as the guiding motif for the introduction. This has the advantage of binding together the Introductory Rite, introducing some unity into this part of the Mass.
- In celebrations where the entrance antiphon is not sung, the incorporation of some of its imagery into the introduction is a way of preserving this traditional part of the liturgy. Most of the antiphons are drawn from the psalms, and offer

many approaches to this important moment of gathering in the presence of God.

- Many presiders include words of welcome. Some commentators point out, however, that it is incongruous to welcome people to their own house and to their own celebration. Ideally, all the participants will have communicated a sense of mutual welcome by the friendly, hospitable way in which they have gathered.
- When introducing the Penitential Rite, it is useful to remember that what is intended here is not a lengthy examination of conscience, but simply a brief acknowledgement that we are sinners.
- The Missal envisages that there will be some occasions when the introduction might be given by someone other than the presider.
- It is a real temptation to try to say too much. The use of too many words can obscure the depths of the mystery we celebrate. Silence is golden.

Allow for Silence

People who are close often speak more deeply through silence than through words. The same can be true of the silence of God and our silence. Heart speaks to heart, sometimes in word, gesture and song, sometimes in stillness and quiet.

The Opening Prayer of the Mass is one occasion when we are invited to enter into a moment of silent prayer. Indeed, one could say that the 'prayer' in this instance is not the text that is read out, but the silent prayer which precedes it. It has been suggested that the word 'Collect', used traditionally to describe the spoken text, refers to the 'gathering together' of all unspoken prayer of the congregation.

It makes sense then to have a real pause for prayer after the invitation 'Let us pray'. Allow time for people to pray. Let the silence be palpable.

Use the Most Evocative of All Our Bodily Senses

One of the main elements of liturgical renewal since Vatican II has been the provision of a wider selection of readings from sacred scripture. Another vitally important change has been the translation of liturgical texts into the vernacular. Human experience teaches however that words are often not enough, especially if we are dealing with matters that are intensely significant. There are moments in life when the body comes to the rescue, in order to help us with our words. A kiss, an embrace, a handshake, a pat on the back or a clenched fist will often add greater power to what we are trying to say. One of the strengths of good Catholic liturgy is that it recognises the importance of the body in worship. Through eating and drinking, washing and anointing, walking, singing, bowing and a host of other bodily activities, the word of God and our human response are embodied. A simple tool for examining our liturgies and improving them is to ask these very simple questions: What do I see? What do I hear? What do I taste? What do I touch? What do I smell?

The use of incense involves seeing and smelling, and indeed sometimes hearing the clink of the chains of a thurible. The rising smoke has often been seen as symbolic of prayer. Incense has been used for centuries as a sign of honour, adoration and purification. It's not just about smoke but, more importantly, about perfume. The sense of smell is often forgotten about in liturgical preparation, although it is probably the most evocative of all the senses. We have all had the experience of walking into a building or a room and smelling something that brings us back years, if not decades, even right back to our childhood. The sense of smell and the working of the memory are closely connected in the human brain. In many parishes incense is now only used at funerals. It would be a terrible pity if it were to become a reminder of death and nothing more. While some care is needed in relation to health issues (for example not using too much incense in a confined space), there is room for using it more regularly at Sunday Mass. Liturgy works better when it involves all the senses.

One of the central insights of the liturgical theology of Vatican II is the manifold presence of Christ in the liturgy: present in the assembly, in the proclamation of the scriptures, in the priest and in the eucharistic species. In a sense one could build up a whole programme of liturgical renewal around a reawakening of sensitivity to each of these ways in which Christ is present. It is interesting that the traditional moments of incensation in the Mass correspond to these different modes of presence: incensation of the altar, the Book of Gospels, the priest, the people and the eucharistic species. Often we tend to go for an all or nothing approach to the use of incense. In other words, we either use incense at all these moments or we do not use it at all. We should feel free to use incense even at one or two moments, as the emphasis of a particular liturgy suggests. One could also have a plan of 'progressive solemnity' which reserves the full use of incense for only the more solemn occasions, while it is used to a more limited extent at other times. A liturgy which engages all the senses is more likely to appeal to people at a deeper level than something that relies too heavily on the spoken word.

35

Share Some Tips with Your Parish Readers

Some or all of the following ideas may help:

- Read each day's reading to yourself and ask God to help you to understand it. Is there anything in the text that mirrors something going on in your own life?
- Write out all the verbs in the passage. This can help you to see what is happening in it.
- Are there any people named in the passage? Do you identify with any of them?
- What do you think the most important line in the reading is? Learn it off by heart.
- Read from the Lectionary (the official book of readings), not from a flimsy sheet.
- Before Mass, go to the ambo and check the location of the reading.
- Look at the congregation before you begin to read.
- Allow a pause of about five seconds between saying 'A reading from x' and the actual text of the reading. Similarly, at the end of the reading allow about five seconds between the last word of the reading and the conclusion 'The word of the Lord'.

- There is no need to say 'first reading' or 'second reading'.
- When you proclaim the word of God, speak slightly more slowly and distinctly than you would in ordinary conversation.
- The Lectionary contains a short phrase in *italics*. This phrase is there for you, the reader, to help you to make sense of the reading. It is not there to be read out loud.
- Lots of user-friendly materials are being published all the time about the Bible. Start reading some of these to get a better grasp of the Bible as a whole and the ways in which God speaks to us through human words and history. Ask your local priest for some help in choosing the right material if necessary.
- Whenever you come across a line in a reading that really speaks to your heart, write it down and treasure it for the rest of your life.
- If you are proclaiming the first reading at Mass, you may find it helpful to use the responsorial psalm as a prayer through the week (or just a line or two from it). The psalm picks up the theme of the reading in a prayerful way.

Bless Your Parish Readers Publicly to Inaugurate their Ministry

The importance of the ministry of those who proclaim God's word each week has only recently been rediscovered in many Catholic parishes. Much still needs to be done to bring about a better appreciation of this work of service. Ministry of the word is demanding and requires a certain level of skill and preparation. When lay readers reappeared for the first time after Vatican II they were often asked to perform their ministry with little preparation or formal recognition of their role. An increasing number of parishes now have a rite of blessing of new readers, which takes place after a number of preparatory sessions about the ministry in general. The rite need not be elaborate and might best take place at Sunday Mass. Ideally, a day would be chosen where the ministry of the word is highlighted in the content of the readings; for example, a day where we hear the preaching and teaching of Jesus or where the ministry of the word in the Church is mentioned. The rite could take the following form:

- After the Profession of Faith the new readers are called forward.

- They are asked if they are willing to undertake this ministry, and they answer 'I am'.
- The Prayer of the Faithful follows, while the readers remain in the sanctuary
- The intercessions include references to the ministry of the word and to the hearing of the word among the people of God.
- The concluding prayer, read by the priest, includes a blessing of the new readers.
- They are presented with a book of scripture (which need not be expensive, and which could have some appropriate dedication written in the front page).

Honour the Word of God Visually – It Speaks Volumes

A visit to the National Museum in Dublin will reveal priceless treasures of liturgical art: the Ardagh chalice and the Derrynaflan chalice. These eucharistic vessels display a very high standard of metalworking craft and are an eloquent testimony to eucharistic faith. A short distance away in Trinity College, Dublin, is another masterpiece, the Book of Kells. Some of the pen work in this illuminated manuscript is so intricate that it can hardly be seen by the naked eye. This speaks of immense reverence for the scriptures, which are proclaimed in the liturgy as the word of God. The Book of Kells is itself a precious vessel of the word.

We might look at our own scripture books and their quality. A really beautiful Book of Gospels speaks loudly about the value of the message contained therein. It can be carried in the entrance procession and placed on the altar. Later, it is carried in procession to the ambo, kissed and incensed. After the proclamation of the gospel, a suitable place can be found for the book: some churches have an ambo designed with a shelf on the front so that the book can be displayed open, others have a special shrine of the gospel where people can come to read and pray after the liturgy, or the book can be returned to the altar and left there until the end of Mass.

The ambo itself also needs to be considered. Is it truly worthy of the proclamation of the word of God? Is it masked by banners? Is its importance lessened by the presence of a second 'ambo' in front of the presider's chair? Is it large enough to accommodate three readers for the reading of the Passion?

The Second Vatican Council proclaimed, 'The Church has always venerated the divine scriptures as she venerated the Body of the Lord.' Let's make sure that this is visible in the choice of furnishings we use for the Liturgy of the Word.

Look at All the Factors that Communicate the Power of God's Word

The readings of the third Sunday in Ordinary Time (Year C) speak of the power of God's word and a humble attitude towards it. When Ezra the priest proclaimed from the Book of the Law people listened attentively. It was read from a special elevated platform. Upon hearing the word, people prostrated themselves to the ground – the meaning of the message was explained and must have pierced people to the heart because they were in tears as they listened. When Jesus read from the scroll of the prophet Isaiah, the true meaning of the scriptures became clear – they were about him and were being fulfilled even as he spoke.

The importance of the message of the scripture is not only brought home by clear, informed proclamation and well-prepared preaching. These are indeed vitally important, but also important are the other cues that surround this proclamation: an ambo that is worthy of its function, beautifully made, well lit and that attracts attention naturally; a lectionary that speaks of the importance of the message it contains; a first-rate public address system (if the church is large) with a loop system for those who are hard of hearing. Having the scriptures solemnly carried in the entrance procession also speaks of their importance. Small details indeed, but together adding up to a consistent and important message about the proclaimed word, which is, after all, the foundation upon which the rest of the liturgy is built.

Sing Alleluia, it's So Easy!

'Alleluia!' This joyful acclamation rings out again and again as the light of the risen Lord flashes across the inner landscape of our minds and hearts. It sings of an unearthly radiance that rises like the dawn over the human race. To say 'alleluia' rather than to sing it is as incongruous as reciting the national anthem or reciting 'Happy Birthday'. For this reason the new General Instruction of the Roman Missal says that if the Gospel Acclamation is not sung it may be omitted.

There are many musical settings of the Alleluia which are very easy and fairly well known. One does not need to be a trained singer to start a congregation singing it. The Alleluia is in fact a very good place in the Mass to start if you want to introduce people to singing: it is brief, simple and highlights a climactic moment in the Liturgy of the Word. Many musical versions are so simple that they do not need any instrumental accompaniment. This means that it can be sung at weekday Masses and on other occasions when there are no trained musicians present. It is so short that it does not lengthen the Mass, but it does add a sense of lift and lightness. The first attempts may be very timid and tentative; this does not stop their being very beautiful, not only to our ears but to God's.

Use the Actions and Signs of the Liturgy Itself to Flesh Out the Imagery of the Homily

We have been reasonably good at making the most of the liturgical changes envisaged by Vatican II, but we have done very little about liturgical formation; that is, about helping people to understand more deeply the meaning of the liturgy and the changes that have been made. Another name for this might be 'liturgical catechesis'. The primary purpose of the homily is, of course, not catechetical; there can, however, be a catechetical spin-off.

When homilists try to flesh out the meaning of the gospel message, they are often on the lookout for images, quotations and examples to strengthen the argument. The words and actions of the liturgy itself are a goldmine in this respect. For example, if the message to be preached were about 'sharing', some reference to the meaning of the breaking of bread at Mass would be very appropriate. In this way, liturgical catechesis can be built into the homily without compromising its basic scriptural focus.

Pray with the Body, it's Natural

One of the most powerful tools for prayer given to us by God is our body, and yet it is so often overlooked. A theological wit once coined the phrase 'God's frozen people' as a sad commentary of what God's chosen people are often like in reality. The author of the phrase was perhaps not thinking specifically of the body in liturgy, but somehow the cap fits.

In Ireland we tend to be minimalistic when it comes to prayer of the body. Perhaps we are afraid of empty externalism, but psychologists are increasingly aware of how bodily movement and posture affect the mind. Liturgically speaking, a posture of reverence is likely to bring about an interior attitude of reverence. In the Creed, for instance, the Missal directs us to bow during those extraordinary words about the incarnation of Christ, yet this is rarely observed. It would be an interesting experiment for presiders to begin by making this gesture themselves. Later, if it seems an appropriate development, everyone in the congregation could be encouraged to do likewise.

Write the General Intercessions with Economy and Flair

- The norm is that the Prayer of the Faithful is introduced and concluded by the presider, with the intentions read by a reader. On some occasions, for example at weekday Masses, it may be that everything is read by the presider, but this is not the ideal.
- The basic content of the introduction could be said to be 'Let us pray'. It is an invitation to prayer, addressed to the congregation. It need not be long.
- The scope of prayer should be wide. We are not simply praying for our own needs, but interceding for people everywhere. The traditional structure of prayer – for the Church, for those in civil authority, for those in special need, for the dead – need not be slavishly followed, but it does show a truly universal way of praying. One could adapt an idea from Dietrich Bonhoeffer and say that the prayer of the faithful should be composed 'with the readings in one hand and the newspaper in the other'.
- Don't try to say everything. Too many intentions can become longwinded and tiresome if care is not taken.

- Use language that is simple, clear and beautiful.
- A variety of responses are possible, for example: Lord hear us/Lord graciously hear us, Lord in your mercy/hear our prayer, Let us pray to the Lord/ Lord hear our prayer, Lord have mercy/Lord have mercy.
- A sung response often gives a lift to this form of prayer, which is in danger of becoming dry and heavy-going. A pause for silent prayer is also a very effective response and should be considered.
- Having a large number of readers, one for each intention, is often desirable at international gatherings where many languages are spoken. At a local liturgy it is more likely to be a distraction from the business at hand, which is prayer.
- Don't fall into the trap of using the prayer of the faithful as another moment for preaching or teaching.
- The concluding prayer is addressed to God the Father. Its basic content could be summed up in the words 'hear our prayer'. The text of the readings and the psalm of the day can often inspire beautiful ways of addressing God. The prayer, which is prayed through Christ our Lord, should end with a traditional ending which elicits a response of 'Amen' from the congregation.

Cultivate a Sense of the Altar as a Consecrated Space Set Aside for a Particular Purpose

At the Olympic Games, the top step is reserved for the gold medalist. In the National Concert Hall in Dublin the presidential seats are used by the President of Ireland and no one else. Reserving spaces in this way is a way of showing honour. In the liturgical space of our church buildings, the altar is reserved for the Eucharist. There is a subtle language at work here, which speaks to people even if they do not realise or completely understand it. This is something that liturgical planners and ministers need to be aware of. Even flowers, which are there to decorate the altar, are ideally placed in front or around it rather than on it. Likewise, there is the tradition of having candles around rather than on the altar. The presence of a Missal on the altar is only a concession to cater for the needs of the presider. If there is really need for a microphone, it should be as unobtrusive as possible.

The altar is not envisaged as a 'parking space' for leaflets, church notices, spectacles or their cases, hymn books or other odds and ends. Such items detract from its symbolic power. Nor is it a place for signing civil marriage documents – a suitable table can be found for this. It is not a place for making announcements. It is very rare that the rites of Vatican II envisage anything else being at or on the altar. The Book of Gospels, if it is to be carried in procession to the ambo, is first placed on the altar. This shows the importance of the gospel reading and emphasises the theological unity of word and sacrament in the celebration. Only three other things ever take place at the altar: the exposition of the Blessed Sacrament, the Concluding Rite of infant Baptism (precisely because it points towards the Eucharist) and the signing of vows in a religious or monastic profession (which are seen as joined to the eucharistic offering).

During Mass itself, the altar is normally only used for the liturgy of the Eucharist. This means that the presider's chair needs to be designed and arranged such that it is possible to truly preside from there for the Introductory Rite and the Liturgy of the Word. It is all too easy to begin Mass at the altar and stay there for the whole of the Introductory Rite, but this confuses the physical focus of the various moments of the liturgy. The shift from the Liturgy of the Word to the Liturgy of the Eucharist becomes all the more significant if the altar has been unused prior to this.

Take Time and Care to Make the Transition from Word to Eucharist

Convenience and good celebration do not always make great partners, either in the liturgy or elsewhere. When people are invited to a meal, it is often inconvenient to have to get out the best tableware, but it does make for a better evening. In liturgical matters we often take shortcuts at the expense of good celebration.

On arriving at Mass, we will find in many church buildings that the altar has already been prepared for the Liturgy of the Eucharist, even though the Liturgy of the Word has not yet happened. On the altar we see chalices, dishes, Missal, corporal, purificators and all the other requisites for the Eucharist already in place. This is not what the Missal envisages, but it is convenient.

The transition from the Liturgy of the Word to the Liturgy of the Eucharist is an important moment which is, if one follows the Missal, articulated in the moment of preparation. From the beginning of Mass the altar has already been prepared with cloth and candles. Once the Liturgy of the Word is over, things move up a gear: the corporal is spread out on the altar, the Missal, chalice, water and purificator are put in place. Only when this is done are the gifts of bread and wine received from the people. All this says quite simply and eloquently that an important moment of the liturgy is about to unfold. Convenience may make the celebration slightly shorter, but it often makes it more boring and overlooks simple opportunities to articulate more clearly the meaning of what is happening.

Give Only Real Gifts at Mass

In the early Roman liturgy people brought gifts of food to Mass and presented them along with the bread and wine. This was an expression of solidarity with those in need and made good theological sense. Real gifts, generously given, together with the bread and wine, speak of the self-donation that is at the heart of the Eucharist: Christ's gift of himself and our self-giving in return. The language of real gifts speaks much louder than symbolic 'tokens', given only to be taken back again at the end of Mass.

If a collection is taken up at Mass, it makes sense to do this after the Prayer of the Faithful and to wait for it to be completed before the Procession of Gifts so that it can be brought forward as a gift. In our throwaway culture there may well be many other gifts that could be collected and given to those in need. These too can be carried in procession. The local Society of St Vincent de Paul may be able to advise as to what is helpful. Gifts other than the bread and wine are carried to the sanctuary and placed in a suitably discreet location. Only the bread and wine are brought to the altar itself.

Watch Your Body Language

Body language matters. It has been shown that when discussions or debates take place on television between, for example, opposing politicians, viewers are more influenced by what they see of the debaters than by the arguments they actually propose. This happens without the viewers' awareness. This suggests that presiders in the liturgy should also think about the language their own bodies speak during the celebration.

One example is the way in which the gifts are handled. At the Preparation of Gifts they are held slightly above the altar while the accompanying prayers are said, either in silence or aloud. It is clear that the Missal does not intend a grand gesture of offering before God at this point. The prayers themselves suggest that what is happening is a simple recognition of the gifts we have received from our creator, in preparation for the eucharistic offering. The bodily gesture is thus rather discreet.

The Holy Gifts are held up a second time, each one separately, as the institution narrative unfolds and concludes during the Eucharistic Prayer. The meaning of this gesture is about showing the sacred species to the people. Traditional devotional pictures to do with the Eucharist and the ordained priesthood often show the priest elevating the host or chalice aloft, even above his head, in a way that suggests a sacrificial offering before God. Yet this is misleading – the raising of the gifts above head height was necessitated in the old liturgy because the priest had his back to the people. The gesture was then, as it is now, about showing something sacred to the people and the manner in which the gifts are shown is about visibility.

A third elevation takes place as the final doxology is sung or said. This is the true moment when the gifts are held aloft before God, for it is through, with and in Christ that glory is given to the Father. This suggests that this elevation is the climactic one. It should also continue during the singing of the Great Amen which follows, otherwise the signal given is that the people's response does not really count. In terms of body language, the movement from the Preparation of Gifts to the institution narrative to the doxology and amen is one of *crescendo*. Observing this is a simple, almost subliminal, way of articulating the meaning of the flow of the liturgy.

Know Who You Are Talking To

This seems like a good suggestion for most life situations, but it also applies to liturgical celebrations. Presiders sometimes act as if they don't to know whom they are addressing. The most obvious aspect of this is in the homily. It seems obvious that a homily addressed to school children would have to be different to one addressed to students of theology, but there are other aspects of the celebration where this principle is sometimes forgotten. Here are some examples:

The Eucharistic Prayer is recited or sung by the presider in such a way that it is audible and intelligible by the congregation but it is not addressed to the congregation, it is addressed to the Father. This might seem clear, but some presiders feel the need to deliver the text rather like a newscaster, making as much eye contact as possible with the people. During the Eucharistic Prayer the presider should be more like a musician. The musician gives themselves up to the music and thus draws the listeners in; the presider gives himself up to God in prayer and draws the assembly with him. However, the Eucharistic Prayer begins with a dialogue which is addressed directly to the people. Here, as in the other dialogues of the Mass, it would seem that making a strong interpersonal connection with people is important, through eye contact, gesture and tone of voice.

Bless, Break and Share

Asked 'When in the Mass does the breaking of bread occur?' many regular Mass-goers in this country give puzzled or incorrect answers. This may come as some surprise to those who read the New Testament and find the name 'breaking of bread' given to the eucharistic celebration itself. If the breaking of bread is important enough to become a name for the celebration, how is it that it regularly passes unnoticed? This might come as less of a surprise when one realises that many presiders perform this rite while the Sign of Peace is still happening. Others break the host but do not share it.

When symbolic actions are not well performed the language of the liturgy begins to fall flat. The solution that many adopt is to add in long explanations, as if we did not already have enough words. Another equally weak solution is to add in new symbols so that any chance of perceiving the original ones given by Christ is well and truly lost.

Instead of long explanations about community and sharing, banners saying 'One in Christ' or other ritual crutches, let's simply make sure that people see, eat and taste eucharistic bread broken and shared. Nothing can speak louder than that.

Make General Announcements Before the Final Blessing

In the city of Rome it was tradition for the papal celebration of the Eucharist to move from one venue to another. A vestige of this stational liturgy was given in the Tridentine books, the name of the appropriate church being still given in the text. A recent adaptation is the title Stational Mass, given in the current Ceremonial of Bishops to denote solemn celebrations by the diocesan bishop of the Eucharist in various parts of the diocese.

In the old Roman stational liturgy it was traditional for the deacon to announce the venue for the next celebration before the final blessing. This seems to be the best time in the liturgy for the making of announcements. To do so at other moments tends to interrupt the flow of events. The Concluding Rite sends us out to live what we have celebrated. The announcement of various events in parish life at this moment strengthens the sense of mission and the link between liturgy and life.

Use the Announcements at the End of Mass to Link the Readings and the Mission of Those Who Celebrate

Many liturgical commentators point out the link between the word 'mass' and the word 'Mission'. 'Mass' is the translation of the word *missa*, which means 'sent'. It makes sense then that the Concluding Rite of the Mass might include some missionary dimension about living the mysteries we have celebrated.

Some of the texts of the optional solemn blessing bring out the dimension of liturgy lived. A further option is the possibility of making parish announcements at this time of the Mass. This is the moment provided in the Missal for making brief announcements. If such announcements were made in a language that recalled the Liturgy of the Word of that particular day, then the links between liturgy and life would be further strengthened. The emphasis on brevity is good – there is always the danger of launching into yet another homily. A few well-crafted words, linked both to the readings and to parish activities, could be very helpful.

Occasionally Use Those Solemn Blessings at the End of Mass That Highlight a Sense of Mission

We should leave the church building with a sense of mission, of being sent to live what we have just celebrated. On special occasions the inclusion of one of the solemn blessings in the Missal can heighten this sense, as many of them call down God's blessing on our daily living. These blessings take two forms. One form has three short blessings, to which people answer 'Amen'. Since the texts of these are many and can vary in length, people are sometimes hesitant about saying the 'Amen' response. If this is the case, then the other format may be better: a single, longer prayer, which ends 'through Christ our Lord'. This ending gives a clear cue and always produces the appropriate response.

When People Are Dismissed at the End of Mass, Let Them Go

Picture for a moment the following familiar scenario: at the end of Mass we hear the words 'Go in peace'. Then the choir and organist start into a recessional hymn. About a third of the congregation leave the building, while the others stay on to join in the singing. Those who have remained may even feel slightly superior. They are, of course, wrong. The liturgy ended with the dismissal and the words 'Thanks be to God'. The priest said 'Go in peace', and those who left the building are only doing what he proposed. Those who remain on to sing are in fact doing something that is not envisaged in the Mass of the Roman Rite. There is, of course, nothing wrong with singing after Mass, but there is definitely something wrong if the assembly is divided into the 'pass' group and the 'honours' group.

A silent ending seems inappropriate on Sundays and other festive occasions. A better solution is to have some festive instrumental or choral singing as people disperse. Some of the congregation may sit and listen for a while. This solution has a number of advantages: it is true to the ritual plan given in the Missal, it highlights other moments as being more important, it indicates more clearly when the liturgy ends, it avoids any odious divisions and comparisons among the congregation and it presents the music group with a weekly opportunity to perform pieces that cannot be used at moments requiring congregational singing.

Be Mindful of Your Word Count

Pay attention to your word count! Our liturgies are often heavy with words. We introduce everything. We explain everything. We add extra bits into prayers. We moralise and elaborate. No wonder people can become distracted. Let's go for words that are carefully crafted and honed down. Let's allow the symbols of the liturgy to puzzle and intrigue, like the parables in the gospels. Let's allow some delicious moments of silence to creep in.

Model Appropriate Attitudes

Whether they like or not, those who preside at the Eucharist represent role models for all the other members of the assembly. A priest who is prayerful and dignified will call forth similar attitudes among his fellow worshippers. A priest who sings (even if he doesn't sing well) will encourage the people to sing. A priest who listens to the scriptures as they are proclaimed will encourage others to listen. When the presider is rushed, ill-prepared or superficial in his manner, he need not be surprised to find something of the same approach developing in his congregation. Here is a simple formula for presiding: ask yourself what attitudes you would like to see at work in your congregation, then start putting them into practice yourself.

Look Out for Children at Mass

The presence of children at Sunday Mass presents a particular pastoral challenge and opportunity. If nothing in the liturgy speaks to them there arises the danger that they are not being well prepared for a life-long commitment to the central act of worship of the Christian week. On the other hand, the Sunday liturgy belongs to everyone, and should not be adapted to such an extent that it speaks to only one group within the parish. The following suggestions may point to a balanced approach:

- Some portion of the homily could address the children directly.
- Children could be involved in bringing forward the gifts of bread and wine.
- Before the final blessing there could be another brief word to the children, reminding them of what they have celebrated and encouraging them to live accordingly.

These three suggestions certainly do not represent the full range of what could be done but they are simple enough to be implemented at any liturgy, even at short notice, and not just at what is referred to a Children's Mass or Family Mass.

Have a Special Liturgy of the Word for Children When They Attend Sunday Mass in Large Numbers

When large numbers of children are present at Sunday Mass certain adaptations can be made to the liturgy for their benefit. The challenge is to strike the balance between suitable adaptation and preserving a liturgy that is for all. The Directory on Masses with Children allows for a radical solution when these conflicting needs seem irreconcilable: the children are taken to a separate place for the Liturgy of the Word and return to the main assembly for the Liturgy of the Eucharist. This solution is not without its critics, who say that it is fundamentally not a good idea to divide the liturgical assembly. It does, nonetheless, also have its advocates. The following ideas may help those who wish to try this option.

- At the end of the Introductory Rite, the children can be led in procession from the main assembly.
- It is important that their own Liturgy of the Word is a true liturgy and not a classroom experience.
- In the place where they will celebrate the word it would be appropriate to have the book of

scriptures enthroned on a stand or table, with lighted candles around it.

- When it comes to hearing the word of God, quality of communication is more important than quantity of readings or of scripture verses.
- While storytelling and explanation of the scriptures are important, it is a good idea to always include a proclamation for the scripture text itself, and not just a paraphrase. It would be good to introduce and conclude the scripture reading(s) with the traditional responses so that the children become familiar with them. Likewise, they would do well to adopt the usual postures for the respective readings.
- Reading, singing, praying and silence are all important. Other creative activities, such as drawing and writing, might be possible but only if they can be really integrated into the worship experience.
- It would be helpful to establish a regular pattern to the celebration so that the children know to some extent what to expect.
- When the Liturgy of the Word is over, the children can be led into the main assembly again to the accompaniment of song or other music. They could quite naturally continue the movement of their procession by bringing up the gifts.

Involve Children in the Processions of the Sunday Liturgy

Children can find it hard to sit still at Mass. The idea of remaining stationary in a wooden pew is a relatively late invention, with its origins in the Protestant Reformation. Living liturgy tends to involve movement of some form or other.

A simple way to involve children in the physical movement of the liturgy is to look at the various processions that are in the rites. Have them process into the church together with the priest and other ministers at the beginning of the Mass. If some are old enough to carry candles, involve them in a procession with the Book of Gospels during the singing of the Alleluia. Make provision for involving a number of children in the Procession of Gifts by ensuring that *all* the bread and wine is carried in procession (we should be doing this anyway). The movement towards the altar for the reception of Holy Communion is also envisaged traditionally as a procession. Thought might be given to finding some ways of ensuring that it is perceived as a procession and not just a queue.

Cleanse the Sacred Vessels Unobtrusively

The table of the Lord is a sacred place for the eucharistic banquet. Through sharing the one bread and the one cup we participate in the sacrifice of Christ. In this sense the table is also symbolically an altar. Anything done at this altar is of great significance: in solemn celebrations, the placing of the Book of Gospels, the Preparation of the Gifts, the Eucharistic Prayer, the breaking of bread and the rites that surround it.

By contrast, the cleansing of vessels after Holy Communion is a relatively insignificant activity and is best done away from the altar, even after Mass is over. In this way the truly important actions stand out all the more clearly and this is communicated to participants, even if only at an unconscious level.

Have Some Singing at Weekday Masses

An increasing number of parishes around Ireland are introducing some singing into weekday Masses. This is very much in line with the thinking of the new General Instruction of the Roman Missal, which sees Masses without singing as something abnormal. This applies even to weekday Masses.

It is not a matter of trying to introduce a number of hymns into the liturgy. A few decades ago that approach had been irreverently nicknamed the 'four-hymn sandwich' – music was generally added in at four points, namely Entrance, Offertory, Communion and Recessional. Adding in hymns in this manner requires hymn books and does not really correspond to best liturgical practice. The 'four-hymn sandwich' is singing at Mass; what the revised liturgy envisages is singing the Mass , or at least singing some parts of it. At a weekday Mass in is often only realistic and suitable to sing one or two important parts of the Mass. A simple formula would be to sing three items: (1) a simple Alleluia before the gospel; (2) a simple setting of the acclamation after the consecration; and (3) a simple setting of the 'Lamb of God'. Singing these three items has the effect of highlighting very significant and important moments within the liturgy. The pieces are short, the words are known and there are some simple settings which are now known in virtually every parish in the country. There is no need for a choir or organist. Anyone with a half-decent voice can start the piece off. The 'Lord have mercy' and the Great Amen are also short simple pieces that can be sung easily.

It doesn't take much to build up a simple repertoire of short pieces such as those above, which can be sung each day at Mass. On those occasions when there is a funeral at Mass it also means that there will be a minimum amount of singing, and should there be a soloist present, a certain minimum of congregational singing will balance out any undue emphasis on solo performance.

60

Use the Summer to Build Up Congregational Singing

As people go away on summer breaks, it may be a good time to look at congregational singing again. The singing of the choir and the singing of the congregation are not mutually opposed; the choir supports the congregation and leads it, as well as singing music of its own. If the choir take some weeks off it does offer the opportunity to let the people hear themselves singing on their own. One or two very simple items may be enough to instil some confidence, which will bear fruit when the choir returns to enhance the liturgy. A cantor can help people to sing when there is no choir.

Involve Singers From Other Parish Choirs

During the summer, when parish choirs are depleted by members going on holidays, the usual response is to disband for a month or two. There is another solution. With many visitors in our parishes during this time of the year, we can always invite those who are members of parish choirs in their home parishes to join with the local choir and augment the numbers. It could make for interesting comparisons, exchanges and contacts, even if the music might be a little less secure.

Celebrate the Sacrament of Baptism Occasionally During Sunday Mass

There is a growing understanding in pastoral liturgy that the celebration of Baptism is a community event, not a private family occasion. Many parishes have Baptism preparation teams: trained lay people who visit the families and help them prepare for the celebration. In some places there is also a meeting for parents in advance of the celebration in order to give them support and deepen their sense of what they are about.

Given the changing patterns of faith and religious practice, it is rare nowadays for parents to simply book a time for a Baptism and turn up on the day. One way of increasing the community profile of Baptism is to incorporate it into Sunday Mass. It need not extend the liturgy unduly. The Welcoming Rite at the door replaces the normal Penitential Rite of the Mass. Since there is a special Profession of Faith, it would make sense to leave out the Creed on this occasion. The short Litany of the Saints and intercessions would also replace the Prayer of the Faithful. The rediscovery of the importance of Baptism is a vital part of liturgical and ecclesial renewal in our time.

Give the Sacrament of Baptism a Higher Public Profile

As well as incorporating Baptism into the Sunday Mass as a way of expressing the important community dimension of this sacrament, other simple things will also help:

- Include a prayer for those to be baptised in the General Intercessions at Sunday Mass.
- Ring the church bells before the celebration itself as a signal to the parish that something important is happening in the church.
- Publish the names of the newly baptised in your parish newsletter.
- Invite families of those newly baptised to an annual celebration – perhaps for the feast of the Baptism of the Lord or during the Easter season.
- If you have more than one choir or music group in the parish ask them to take turns sending a delegation to perform at the celebration of Baptism.
- Have a critical look at the size and location of your baptismal font: does it communicate a sense of the

centrality of Baptism to the Christian life or does it speak of something marginal? Are there any improvements that could be made?

Get People Moving in the Celebration of Baptism

The use of pews for the accommodation of worshippers in Christian liturgy is a relatively late invention, stemming from the Protestant Reformation. Like stalls in cinemas and theatres, pews are for those who listen and watch in a mostly passive mode. But liturgy is an action, not just something listened to or watched. An example of this can be found in the liturgy of Baptism.

In many parishes when people arrive for a Baptism they take their places in pews near the font and remain sitting there for the whole celebration. Other parishes open up the liturgical space, as suggested in the ritual book. The celebration begins at the door for the Introductory Rite, moves to the ambo for the Liturgy of the Word, to the font for the Liturgy of Baptism and concludes at the altar, bringing out the eucharistic orientation of Baptism. This has been described as a 'stational' approach rather than a 'stationary' approach. It involves three processions, from one station to the next. It brings out the journey aspect of the Christian vocation and articulates more clearly the successive stages of the rite. It also engages people in a more active, bodily way. Remaining stationary is easier but speaks less of the adventure of the Christian life and reinforces a passive approach to Church, community and sacrament.

Think About the Size and Position of the Baptismal Font

The order in which things are mentioned in Church documents is rarely accidental. When it comes to Baptism, the pouring of water is mentioned but Baptism by immersion is given as the first option. Those who have been to the baths at Lourdes have some inkling of how powerful a sign this can be. Some people might be worried by the safety of immersing infants in the font, but it is completely safe, and has been the normal method for Baptism in the Orthodox Church for centuries.

Providing for immersion means having bigger baptismal fonts, especially now that the Baptism of adults is becoming a much more frequent event. A larger-sized font is entirely suitable, as the font needs to be one of the outstanding features in any parish church. On the level of symbol, pouring water speaks of washing but little else and tends to reinforce a perspective which limits the meaning of Baptism to the washing away of original sin. Being plunged into the water and coming back up again speaks of death and resurrection. The font becomes both tomb and womb, a place of death and a place of new creation.

In some parishes the font is positioned near the door of the church. This says something of Baptism as the gateway to sacramental life. The font is then also used by people for blessing themselves as they walk into the church – when they dip their hands into the font they are, in a certain sense, touching again the waters of their own Baptism.

Make Sure that Exposition of the Blessed Sacrament Retains Some Relationship to the Celebration of Mass

Exposition of the Blessed Sacrament is one aspect of devotion that merits thoughtful consideration. The official texts dealing with exposition emphasise that there should be a perceptible link between the exposed sacrament and the celebration of Mass. This means, for example, that the usual place for the exposed sacrament is the altar of celebration, rather than some elevated pedestal or niche. The most familiar manner of exposing the Blessed Sacrament is in a monstrance, but the rite also speaks of exposing it by placing an open ciborium on the altar. This alternative would make clearer the link between exposition and the celebration of the Eucharist. The use of a ciborium (*cibum* = food) brings out more clearly the meal aspect of the Eucharist as the fundamental form in which Christ reveals his sacrificial presence.

If Benediction takes place, the blessing itself is the last action of the celebration, forming its conclusion. This means that the Divine Praises or other traditional prayers should be recited before the blessing. This represents a shift of emphasis from the ritual before Vatican II, which is now on exposition, not benediction, of the Blessed Sacrament.

Use This Traditional Template When Writing Prayers

Special occasions often ask for special prayers. Significant moments happen in the lives of communities and individuals that need to be celebrated and explicitly named as part of our pilgrim journey with the Lord. There are many sources we can use and adapt but sometimes the best solution is to write a new prayer. The following suggestions may help.

Begin by naming God
God can be named in many ways: 'Father', 'Eternal Shepherd', 'Saviour', 'Creator' and so on. With a few words one can put together a verbal icon of God as a focus for the praying congregation. The psalms are full of poetic images of God. Let us imagine that we are writing a prayer for a family moving into a new home: one might begin 'O God, our refuge'.

Continue by remembering the words and deeds of God
A key insight of the Judeo-Christian tradition is that God is intimately involved in our lives and in the history of the world. By remembering the events of our own lives, together with the words and events that have been

treasured in the Bible, we get a much fuller picture of this God to whom we are praying. We begin to acknowledge a real, living presence. And so our prayer could read as follows:

O God, our refuge,
you have made your home among us in Christ Jesus,
and have promised to dwell with us for ever.

Ask for what you need
The God who has done great things for us in the past remains unchanged in loving attention and wishes to lavish new gifts on us. Having acknowledged in a small way the gifts of the past we ask for new blessings. Thus the prayer text develops:

O God, our refuge,
you have made your home among us in Christ Jesus,
and have promised to dwell with us for ever.
Enfold N. and N. in your kindness as they move into their new home.
May they make it a place of companionship and forgiveness,
a house of welcomes and a school of love.

Conclude by making the prayer through Christ
Our Christian worship is through Christ, with him and in him. It is traditional to acknowledge this at the end of the prayer and to elicit the response 'Amen'. One can simply say 'Through Christ our Lord'. Sometimes it is desirable to develop this line a little by saying something about who Jesus is to us. He is our resurrection, he is our Saviour, our teacher, our priest, our brother, etc. If the last line is developed it is important to conclude it with a recognisable ending which elicits an 'Amen'. And so our prayer concludes:

O God, our refuge,
you have made your home among us in Christ Jesus,
and have promised to dwell with us for ever.
Enfold N. and N. in your kindness as they move into their new home.
May they make it a place of companionship and for-giveness,
a house of welcomes and a school of love.
Through Jesus Christ, in whom we have become one body,
our Lord, for ever and ever.
Amen.

Do One Thing at a Time

Christian liturgy often combines words and actions to highly significant effect. Pouring water or submerging in water takes on a new meaning when accompanied by the words 'I baptise you ... '. Putting ointment on someone's forehead has a special significance when accompanied by the words 'Be sealed with the gift of the Holy Spirit'.

Sometimes ritual actions are accompanied by song, with a similar effect. A procession with palm branches, when accompanied by the appropriate song, is clearly seen as a way of honouring Jesus as our Messiah. Thus the liturgy often combines disparate elements quite deliberately in order to achieve a certain effect. It is, however, a good liturgical principle that apart from these very specific instances it is not a good idea to do two things at the one time. Some examples may illustrate the point. The collection of money or other goods has long been a feature of liturgical celebrations but it should not happen while other liturgical actions unfold; for example, during the Creed, the Prayer of the Faithful, the Preparation of the Gifts or, worse still, during a scripture reading or the Eucharistic Prayer. It is not good liturgy for a presider to dialogue with the people (e.g. 'The Lord be with you') and at the same time hunt around for the page of the preface. It is not a good idea to read notices during the time of prayer after Holy Communion. Each liturgical action works best when it is allowed to stand in its own space and time.

Re-examine the Entrance Procession for Weddings

Most engaged couples are quite happy with the traditional procession of the bride, whereby she is led by one man, normally her father or elder brother, and 'given away' to another, namely the groom. They accept this while more than likely rejecting the message it actually communicates about the place of women in family life. Such a procession need not take place from a liturgical point of view. At some weddings both bride and groom process in together, with or without parents. The priest and other ministers may also be part of the procession. This is one moment when a couple can be helped to arrive at a more thoughtful choreography of the entrance rite.

Think Creatively About the Seating Arrangements at Weddings

At many wedding celebrations the bride, groom and attendants sit, stand and kneel in a long line in front of the altar. This is only one possible layout. Sometimes it actually hinders a proper view of the liturgical action. Seating the wedding party sideways or diagonally is also possible.

Nor does the couple have to sit in the place where they will exchange their vows. When it comes to the actual marriage vows it is often suitable for the couple to face one another rather than stand with their backs to the congregation. The splitting of the congregation into two groups related to bride and groom respectively is also a practice that has little support in good liturgical theology, where the unity of all the baptised is something to be expressed and symbolised by seating and layout.

Display the Holy Oils Used in Our Sacraments

For some time now gift shops have recognised the value and popularity of perfumed oils. Such oils soothe, heal and refresh. Yet in the Church we have, by and large, tended to move in the opposite direction: although oils are solemnly blessed each year for the use in sacraments and sacramentals, we use them in amounts so small as to be barely perceptible and often store them in places that say nothing about their dignity. We rarely speak about oil, so that people might be forgiven if they were unaware of its importance when we dab it on. There is the venerable tradition of the aumbry, a properly designed place where the oils are kept in the church building. In some parishes the aumbry is designed so that the oils are beautifully displayed. Since two of the oils are used in Baptism, it makes sense to place the aumbry near the font. This can become a beautiful visual reminder of the use and meaning of oil in our liturgies and a natural focus for catechesis.

Rethink the Timing of the Sacrament of the Anointing of the Sick

For many people the Anointing of the Sick is a sign of approaching death. 'Send for the priest' still has an ominous ring about it. In the early centuries of the Church, anointing of the sick was not confined to the moment we now associate with the 'last rites'. Through various accidents of history, however, the rite became a deathbed sacrament, and has remained so for most people despite the renewed vision of the sacrament at Vatican II.

In the reformed rite of anointing, this celebration is envisaged as appropriately celebrated at the onset of serious illness, and may also be repeated as an illness progresses. Celebrating the sacrament in this way helps people to see *viaticum* (Holy Communion for the dying) as the primary sacrament for the dying. It also allows for a fuller, richer celebration while the patient is still well enough to appreciate its various dimensions.

Use the Opportunities for Catechesis on Anointing of the Sick That Arise in the Sunday Readings

The most suitable place for this celebration is more logically at the onset of serious illness, not at the end of it. It exists to help people through the pain and isolation involved in illness, strengthening their faith precisely at the moment when it may be seriously challenged. This, however, needs to filter into ordinary pastoral practice and thinking. Perhaps one way to do this is to look out for those Sundays where the gospel focuses on illness. This would be an opportunity for some catechesis and discussion.

Have Regular, Communal Celebrations of the Sacrament of the Sick

The Sacrament of Anointing of the Sick is often associated with the deathbed. The principal sacramental celebration for the dying however is *viaticum*, the reception of the Holy Eucharist. Since the sacrament of anointing is concerned with illness and not just with death, the most suitable time for its celebration is the onset of illness, not its termination in death. This also takes the sacrament out of the emergency situation into a context where its celebration can be more dignified and meaningful. It also makes the possibility of a communal celebration where many sick people are together a more real option. Some parishes have the celebration of this sacrament as a communal event at regular intervals, even once a month. This doesn't mean that the sacrament won't also be celebrated in the emergency situation and close to the moment of death, but it begins to place it in a better context from both an ecclesial and a personal point of view.

Ensure That the Anointing of the Sick, Even in its Most Abbreviated Form, is Still a Moment of Faith and Prayer

The Sacrament of the Anointing of the Sick is a liturgical celebration. However, there are occasions when it needs to be fairly short and simple, depending on the condition of the sick person and other factors. Of course it is appropriate to adapt what it is in the ritual book to suit the occasion. It may also be helpful to consider that in good liturgical celebrations, certain elements are normally found and should be included if at all possible in the celebration of anointing, even if in an abbreviated form:

- Gathering of Christians: Ideally there are more than the priest and the sick person present.
- Variety of ministry: Involving family members or other carers even very simply in the rite can be pastorally very effective.
- Hearing of the word of God: In this instance it may only be a well-chosen sentence or two. Remember that for the dying, the ability to hear is often present almost up to the end, even if they are unable to respond.

- Prayer of faith: Such prayer may be brief and pure; but there should be prayer.
- Generous use of symbols: More than a perfunctory dab of oil is recommended. It is an ointment and can be applied like any other ointment.

Express God's Loving Initiative in the Sacrament of Reconciliation

The shepherd goes out in search of the lost sheep. The woman searches for her coin. The father awaits the return of the son and runs out to greet him. When it comes to reconciliation, God makes the first move. It would be most appropriate if this divine initiative were also to be expressed in the Sacrament of Reconciliation and, in fact, it is.

In the pre-Vatican II celebration of the sacrament, the penitent began, 'Bless me Father, for I have sinned'. The new rite now places the initiative with the priest, who greets and welcomes the penitent. Admittedly, when penitents who are used to celebrating the old way present themselves in the accustomed manner, it would not be suitable to interrupt them. When the opportunity presents itself, however, a warm initiative from the confessor corresponds to the thinking behind the rite and expresses a deeper theological truth. When the sacrament is celebrated this way, the possibility of people not knowing what to do at confession is precluded, as the priest is already leading them step by step.

Prepare a Worthy Liturgical Space for the Sacrament of Reconciliation

The importance of the 'seal of confession' indicates the need for the proper soundproofing of the place where it happens. The particular nature of individual confession of sin also calls for other special considerations: the possibility of anonymity should the penitent desire it, the use of a grille should the penitent wish to be hidden from view, and the need for some external visibility should face-to-face confession take place. It is possible to design reconciliation rooms that satisfy all these requirements in a way that allows for both face-to-face confession and a more anonymous manner of interaction. But the design of this space needs to take into account much more than the need for proper boundaries, confidentiality and security. It should be a place worthy of a sacramental celebration.

One may well ask how many of our confession 'boxes' convey the warmth and the love of the Prodigal Father, whose door is open to welcome the erring child. Surely our reconciliation space should speak of light, welcome, peace, compassion and forgiveness! Since the proclamation of a short reading from scripture is also envisaged, a place for the book of scripture could be envisaged. An appropriate icon, well placed and beautifully lit, would also add to the sense of occasion. It is true that less people go to confession nowadays but is it not also true that many of our church buildings tell them that they are not welcome anyway?

Think About Sacramental 'Aftercare'

We tend to put a lot of effort into preparing children for the sacraments but not so much into 'aftercare'. There is a sense, of course, that all catechetical work is feeding into the question of how we live the sacraments we have received. Nonetheless, there is something to be said for gatherings and events which help our children reflect, in a manner appropriate to their age, on what has happened. The traditional word for this is 'mystagogy'. Some of the greatest catechetical texts of history have been born in that moment when the newly initiated were helped to understand the meaning of all that they have been through. The Sacrament of Confirmation might be a good place to start.

Some time after Confirmation it might be good to invite children who have been confirmed to a gathering that is partly celebration, partly catechesis and partly offering them some opportunities for service in the parish. One can presume that the response to this will be much smaller than the number of children actually confirmed, but this doesn't mean that it's not a worthwhile venture.

In the gospels we see time and time again that small beginnings can have long-term results of enormous consequence.

Use Appropriate Rites for the Moment After Death and Raise Awareness in the Month of November

The Sacrament of the Anointing of the Sick is for the sick and dying, not for the dead. We all know that but every now and then pastors are faced with grieving family members requesting that their deceased loved one be anointed. This is understandable: they feel powerless in the face of death and they want to do their best for the person who has died. Traditionally some leeway has been given in such circumstances. It is not always easy to pinpoint the moment of death. Someone may appear to be dead and yet be alive. Conditional anointing is sometimes possible but we also need to start pointing people in another direction.

Drawing attention to the fact that the Anointing of the Sick includes prayers for recovery may help the bereaved realise that this sacrament is no longer suitable. Both the Rite of Christian Funerals and the Pastoral Care of the Sick have special rites drawn up for use just after the moment of death. One of the attractions of the sacrament of anointing is its physical dimension: the anointing of a body. These other rites also have outward gestures which may be pastorally consoling: the use of holy water, the sign of the cross on the forehead of the deceased, etc.

During November, a natural time for remembering the dead, perhaps some catechesis through the parish newsletter or other means could help shape people's expectations regarding rites around the time of death.

Find a Suitable Place for Mementos of the Dead at Funerals

At funerals the bereaved sometimes like to bring up as offertory gifts various items associated with the person who has died. The desire to remember the dead is a healthy one, all the more so if done through tangible signs. It is, however, debatable as to whether the Preparation of the Gifts is the place for such items. The kinds of gifts envisaged in the Roman rite are, aside from the bread and wine, those things that are taken away and given to the poor or used for the needs of the church.

However, this does not mean that some mementos of the dead need be excluded from the liturgy, if they accord with the reverence the occasion demands. A table suitably placed can be prepared and decorated in advance. 'Suitably placed' might indicate that it would not have the same prominence as the major focal points of the building, such as the altar or the ambo. Mementos could be placed on it either when the coffin is brought into the church or as part of the entrance procession of the Mass.

Find Ways of Acknowledging Death at Funerals

The experts tell us that when somebody close to us dies the first reaction we are most likely to have is denial. This is a defence mechanism which no doubt has its place as an initial way of coping with the trauma, but we need help to move on, to realise that the one we love has actually died. Part of the problem in some Western cultures is that life is lived in denial of death. When bodies are seen laid out in funeral homes they often look better than when the person was alive; when the coffin is lowered into the grave it is immediately covered with a board or cloth, sanitising the whole experience. There are even some places where the coffin is not lowered into the ground until the relatives have left the cemetery.

Good funeral liturgy performs many functions but one of the things it should do is to help people acknowledge that death has actually occurred. Our funeral homilies need to speak of death as well as resurrection. Purple may well be a better colour for vestments at this stage rather than white. When it comes to the moment of burial there is the custom in some places of each person present putting some earth into the grave over the coffin. It may be harrowing but it is healthy nonetheless. Others throw flowers into the grave. At cremations perhaps a similar gesture would be to invite the mourners to sprinkle the coffin with holy water one by one.

Keep Your Local Undertakers Informed of the Best Liturgical Practices in Your Parish

Much of the decision making in families after a death is guided to a large extent by undertakers. They are able to relieve the bereaved of the extra burden of trying to organise everything at a moment when they can feel completely at sea. The first person to help the family in this respect may well be the undertaker, not the priest or any other representative of the parish.

In order for good liturgical practice to be implemented without undue difficulty, it is advisable for the best practices to be suggested at an early stage of planning a funeral. It might be a very good idea for a parish to give local undertakers a standard list of liturgical options. In this way, good practice can be suggested before more problematic suggestions arise.

Give the Bereaved Sample Intercessions as a Template for Use in Preparation for the Funeral

Funerals in this country tend to be arranged at the last minute. Where possible, grieving families like to put their own mark on the liturgy. One example of this is the Prayer of the Faithful: quite often family members will write intercessions of their own. This is not of course without its problems. For one, it will often be the first time that someone has written such prayers and they may be clueless as to how to go about it. Intercessions hastily written by the inexperienced don't always sit well within the liturgy, though in their own way they may speak volumes.

A possible solution might be to offer some kind of a template – some sample prayers with examples as to how they might be adapted. In this way, one can give gentle guidance as well as relieve people who are already overburdened of an additional worry.

Build a Team of Ministers Who Can Assist in the Celebration of Funerals

The care of bereaved families is an important task that takes time. One particular aspect of this is the support and advice they need in preparation for the funeral and their participation. This was traditionally carried out by the local priest, but with fewer priests now in this country the amount of time available to give such care and support is diminishing. The decreasing number of priests is not the only reason for developing a funeral ministry team. Such a team can strengthen a wider network of care and support. The kind of work involved may depend on the situation: visiting those who are bereaved, helping them choose readings and prayers, being at the church to receive them when they arrive, helping them with the placing of Christian symbols on the coffin, as well as guiding and supporting those who have a particular role to play. It may be that in future such well-trained lay people may also be called upon to conduct some of the liturgical services associated with the time of death. Those involved in such important work would need training, not only in liturgical celebration but in the care of the bereaved.

Use the Liturgical Books, Rather than Reduced Pastoral Publications, as the Basic Source for Liturgical Preparation

One of the disadvantages of our present liturgical books is that they can be hard to find your way around. Often a range of options can be given for a particular prayer or rite, whereas in the Tridentine liturgy there was normally only one way of doing things. As a result, publishers often produce slimmer booklets or leaflets aimed not just at the liturgical ministers but also at the congregation. For the Rite of Baptism, for example, there are a number of published versions which give only one option for each part of the rite. This is simple, convenient and user friendly. The problem is that it presumes a 'one size fits all' approach. It cuts out the possibility of a more sensitive tailoring of the liturgical options to the actual situation. There is, for example, a version of the Final Blessing at Baptism which blesses mother, father, grandparents and the rest of the community. But it can arise that the father is absent, particularly if he is not married to the mother. In this situation it is important to know the other versions of the Final Blessing that are available in the liturgical book. When it comes to any liturgical rite, privately produced publications may have their uses, but it is good to go back regularly to the official liturgical text to see all the options. Even after many years of celebration one can discover new possibilities which somehow were not noticed in an earlier context.

Remember the Sense of Touch and Use it Appropriately

A woman attending a funeral turned to an older man sitting nearby at the Sign of Peace and shook his hand. The man burst into tears. The tears were nothing to do with the funeral or the deceased, rather it was because no one had actually touched this man in over a decade.

Touch plays an important part not just in the Mass but in all our sacramental celebrations, and needs to be cultivated. Think of the anointing that happens at Baptism, Confirmation, the Anointing of the Sick and Ordination. Best practice would suggest more than a quick dab of oil. This seems especially important in the Anointing of the Sick, where a therapeutic massaging of oil is part of the underlying symbolism of the rite.

The laying on of hands is also there not just in the sacraments of Confirmation, Anointing of the Sick and Ordination, but also in Reconciliation. Obviously a laying on of hands in a confession box is often impractical or even impossible because of grilles and other barriers (and recent scandals have made us more aware of why such barriers may be in place) and so it is often replaced by a simple lifting up of the hand in the direction of the penitent. In the communal celebration of this sacrament, where the giving of absolution happens 'out in the open', a proper laying on of hands becomes possible and in many instances desirable. Sometimes a hand on the shoulder of the penitent is also a helpful sign of welcome and encouragement.

A very small minority of our congregations object to the Sign of Peace during Mass on grounds of hygiene: one never knows what kind of germs another person may be carrying. Touch is messy, not just biologically but emotionally. It transmits not just germs but emotional overtones, with all the richness and ambiguity implied therein. It is precisely in this 'messiness' of human encounter that the sacraments operate – this is their preferred milieu, their home territory. Let's be wise about healthy boundaries in the area of human touch but let's also make sure not to starve our sacraments of the language of touch.

Look for Opportunities for a People-Friendly Celebration of the Liturgy of the Hours

In recent centuries we have come to think of the Liturgy of the Hours as something primarily, if not exclusively, for priests and religious. We think of priests reciting the breviary on their own and of religious communities celebrating it in common. One of the aims of the liturgical reform after Vatican II was to restore the celebration of the Liturgy of the Hours as a celebration for the people of God as a whole. An increasing number of lay people are discovering the Liturgy of the Hours as a helpful form of personal daily prayer. This is no surprise, as it is largely scriptural and draws particularly on the psalms. Yet this liturgy is primarily a communal celebration and needs to be promoted as such. Historically speaking, it is in fact the older daily liturgy for the community, daily Eucharist being a later development.

With dwindling numbers of ordained priests in Ireland, the daily celebration of the Liturgy of the Hours becomes even more important in a context where daily Mass may no longer be possible in every parish. People often like to take on special spiritual exercises for the seasons of

Advent and Lent. Perhaps next Advent and Lent will be times to launch some form of Liturgy of the Hours for more general use in your parish.

Have a People-Friendly Version of Night Prayer [Compline] Available for Use at Meetings

With busy work schedules, many parish meetings involving groups of parishioners take place at night. In many instances the group will like to begin or end with prayer. Devise a people-friendly booklet of Night Prayer that can be easily handed around at the end of a meeting and used with little hesitation by all present. This will give people a taste for the Liturgy of the Hours in a format that is relatively simple and attractive.

Think Long-Term about Flexible Seating

The architecture and arrangement of the liturgical space in which we gather has a huge effect on the dynamics of worship. Large-scale architectural changes are very expensive, difficult to judge well and sometimes divisive. Still, they are often necessary. One aspect that can be examined within an existing space is the question of seating. The idea that all the congregation need to be locked into rows of benches is a fairly recent phenomenon in the West, and does not represent the majority of liturgical instinct over the centuries.

Given the huge range of liturgical events and widely varying congregations that we have to host in our church buildings, there is a lot to be said for a more flexible form of seating. Flexible seating allows the congregation to take different shapes, depending on the needs of the situation. It allows the possibility of varying the visual focus of the gathering and makes room for movement of various kinds. It also expresses something of the nature of the Church, which is a pilgrim people, continually growing and changing, always in need of reform. For those situations where something like rows of benches seems appropriate, modern church seating has now been designed that can be locked into rows when necessary. You may not be able to do much about the basic structure of your church building but you may be able to open up many new possibilities by rethinking your seating.

Bring the Spirituality of the Liturgy into Daily Life: The Jesus Prayer

Part of good liturgical renewal in our parishes is improving what happens in our liturgy. Another dimension involves looking at how we live our spirituality and tune it more closely to that of the liturgy.

The Penitential Rite of the Mass teaches us something about humility in God's presence. 'Lord, have mercy' is an acknowledgement of the mercy and goodness of Christ; it also expresses our need for help. A way of bringing this outlook into our daily living is to use the Eastern tradition of the Jesus Prayer. The Jesus prayer is a short invocation: 'Jesus, Son of God, have mercy on me, a sinner.' There are some variants in the actual wording of it from place to place. The traditional practice is to repeat this prayer from time to time during the day – sprinkling our daily activities with its wholesome presence. The prayer acknowledges the greatness of who Jesus is: the only Son of God, the one whose name is above every other name, the one through whose name all can be saved. It also cuts through any self-deception by candidly acknowledging that we are all sinners. The attitude of the Penitential Rite can then permeate our day. When we come together and enter into the Penitential Rite as one body, the ongoing practice of the Jesus Prayer makes this moment ring true and echo deeply in our hearts.

Bring the Spirituality of the Liturgy into Daily Life: Personal Engagement With Scripture

The Liturgy of the Word represents a real challenge to many in our congregations. Clearly there is much to be done in terms of homiletics and the training of ministers of the word, but we also need to look at the place of the scriptures in the lives of people outside the liturgy. Is it realistic to expect people to suddenly dip into the scriptures for fifteen minutes each Sunday if they have had no contact with the Bible during the week?

We need to find strategies for bringing the scriptures into daily living. For example, training in *lectio divina*, scriptural suggestions in the parish newsletter and website, Bible study groups, leaflets and books in the church bookshop and talks in the parish from scripture experts.

Bring the Spirituality of the Liturgy into Daily Life: Daily Exercise in Thanksgiving

'Eucharist' means 'thanksgiving'. A eucharistic spirituality should therefore be a spirituality of thanksgiving. This does not come naturally to most people. An attitude of thanksgiving is something that often needs to be learned. If we never give thanks to God during the day or during the week then our daily or weekly Eucharist will seem unreal.

A simple and life-giving exercise that can be done at the end of each day is to think back over the day and replay in one's mind different moments for which one is grateful. No matter how badly a day may seem to have gone, there are always moments for which we can give thanks. Gradually we can learn to be grateful rather than grasping. The words 'it is our duty always and everywhere to give you thanks' may eventually begin to make sense.

Watch Your Clutter

Many a sideboard or mantelpiece at home is cluttered with ornaments and odds-and-ends. Memorabilia and 'things that might come in handy' are rarely thrown out. The same can happen in the interior of our churches. It is a good idea occasionally to do a clutter check of the inside of the church building. You may be surprised to see how the beautiful, clear lines of many a sanctuary, side chapel, church porch or transept are obscured by extra chairs, tables, potted plants, banners, pictures, notices and much more.

Make Sure the Fundamental Symbols of the Liturgy Communicate with Amplitude Before Adding New Ones

There can be a tendency among those who prepare our liturgies to add new symbols while the more fundamental symbols remain mute and largely ignored. Before we consider adding more layers of symbol and explanation, we should ensure that our bread, unleavened though it may be, has the consistency of real food, that the host handled by the priest be large enough to be really broken and shared, that Communion under both kinds be the rule rather than the exception, that someone gets wet when water is sprinkled, that the paschal fire at Easter be something more than a few flames in a tin bucket, that the Cross on Good Friday be of a size and dignity that is worthy of veneration, that the thurible produces perfumed smoke and not just the clank of chains, that the Procession of Gifts really does bring what is required for the Eucharist from among the gather to the altar and not just a minimalist token, and so on.

On Big Occasions Have a 'Master of Ceremonies' Who is Not the Presider

It often falls to the presiding priest to organise the preparations for liturgical celebrations and to see to it that all the details are in place. In many instances this works well. The role of presiding at the church's liturgy is, however, different from that of coordinating and even prompting others who have a particular role to play. On big occasions it is better that someone other than the presider be available to direct the altar servers, readers and others who need help and support in carrying out their respective roles. This leaves the presider free to attend to the needs of the assembly as a whole and to lead them in worship.

Put Together a CD of Suitable Music for Weddings and Funerals

The choice of music for weddings and funerals can be problematic. If those involved are not presented early on with examples of suitable music, less desirable alternatives will often be suggested. Nowadays it is not hard to compile a CD of hymns and songs that are both appropriate and correspond to a variety of musical tastes.

In conjunction with your parish musicians, pick songs you know they can perform and put them on a CD that can be easily copied. At the very first encounter with an engaged couple or a bereaved family, the appropriate CD can be given to them.

If a CD proves impractical, it may be possible to find examples of good liturigal music on the internet and put together a list of links, which people can visit in order to hear the music you are proposing.

When Faced with Requests for Music That is Liturgically Unsuitable, Try to Find a More Suitable Context

Music which cannot be used during Mass or during the Reception of the Body at Funerals may sometimes find a place just outside the boundaries of the liturgy. At weddings the liturgy is over when the bride and groom are signing the register. The same is true of that moment when sympathisers greet a bereaved family before leaving the church. In difficult pastoral situations a concession to the pressures of the moment can be to have non-liturgical music at these moments which are, strictly speaking, non-liturgical. Music which simply should not be heard in church may still find an appropriate point during the larger 'rites' of marriage or death, for example at the wedding reception or during a wake or funeral meal.

Make Sure Your Church Furnishings and Requisites Are Honest

Through the symbolic language of liturgy, the deeper realities of life in God shine forth. This is not helped when the signs used lack authenticity. If it looks like a candle it should be a candle, not a canister of oil enclosed in a fake plastic tube. If it looks like a burning flame it should be a burning flame rather than a flickering bulb. If it looks like a flower it should be a flower. If it sounds like a bell it should be a bell. If it sounds like a pipe organ it should, if you can afford it, be a pipe organ (such instruments do cost more but are never replaced, while their artificial counterparts become obsolete rather like television sets). Not only is there a lack of authenticity about liturgical fakes; nine times out of ten they are unconvincing anyway.

Embrace the Messiness of Processions

We are a pilgrim Church, a people on the move with no lasting city here below. Movement is part of the liturgical experience and expresses our common identity and our solidarity amidst change and development. When Jesus made his great journey to Jerusalem he invited people to 'follow me', and early Christians were known as 'followers of the Way'. Saint John even refers to Jesus himself as 'the Way'. Small wonder then that the Church envisages processions to highlight this dynamic at pivotal moments of the liturgy:

At Baptism
- Procession from the door to the ambo
- Procession from the ambo to the font
- Procession from the font to the altar

At Mass
- The Entrance Procession
- The procession with the Book of Gospels
- The procession with the Gifts
- The procession for Holy Communion

At Funerals
- The processions with the body

During the Liturgical Year

- The procession with candles at the Feast of the Presentation of the Lord
- The procession with Palms on Palm Sunday
- The procession with the Blessed Sacrament on Holy Thursday
- The procession with the Cross on Good Friday
- The procession with the Paschal Candle on Holy Saturday

In addition to these there are sometimes devotional processions, for example:

- Procession to the crib at Christmas
- Processions with the Blessed Sacrament
- Marian processions

Processions are most effective when the whole congregation moves, as was often the case in classic Roman liturgies. Moving a large body of people is messy and demanding. It involves planning, stewarding, even 'crowd control', and in Ireland is further complicated by the vagaries of weather. The temptation always is to 'domesticate' processions by reducing them to a few people, reducing their distance or eliminating them altogether. The popularity of parades and protest marches worldwide suggests that this approach flies in the face of human nature and eliminates a fundamental symbol found in virtually every culture. Catholic liturgy at its best embraces all that is wholesome in human culture, even though it is hard to manage or direct. Let's have the courage to walk together, even if we get a bit lost or muddled along the way.

Using the Rite of Christian Initiation of Adults as a Model, Structure Parish Life Around the Liturgy as its Summit and Source

When adults present themselves as interested in becoming Christians it means:

- They have encountered something in Christianity which attracts and inspires them.
- They are willing to meet others who already live the Christian life.
- They will be helped to interpret their lives through the sacred stories of the Bible.
- They will experience hospitality and encouragement.
- Others will share with them what it means to be a Christian.
- Certain individuals will be asked to support them personally on their journey.
- They will be taught how to pray.
- They will be given reassurance when they are afraid.
- They will encounter the faith not as an abstract set of ideas or rules but as a living reality celebrated

in the liturgical year, proclaimed in the Sunday scriptures and lived in a local community.

- The Sunday lectionary will be the basic guide for their introduction to the faith.
- Various rituals will mark key moments of development in their lives.
- They will experience Lent as a time of purification when the Holy Spirit uncovers for them aspects of their lives that need to be healed.
- Easter will be the high point of their year.
- They will celebrate the sacraments, culminating in the Eucharist, which will remain the weekly renewal of their identity as members of the body of Christ.
- They will be helped to reflect on their experience of the sacraments and to live them more deeply in love of God and neighbour.
- They themselves will become witnesses of Christ's love, through whom others will be drawn into the same mystery, the same journey, the same extraordinary web of relationships.

While certain aspects of the journey of adult initiation happen only once in a lifetime (for example enrolment as catechumens, the rite of election in preparation for Baptism, the sacraments of Baptism and Confirmation), much of it reflects the extraordinarily rich dynamic of a vibrant sacramental life which revolves around the three poles of word, sacrament and Christian living, and as such remains an exciting model for parish life.

Remember That, in the End, Liturgy is More God's Work Than Ours

Those who prepare for our liturgies are serving the whole assembly and their ministers. The liturgy is celebrated by the whole assembly even if certain roles are taken by particular ministers within that assembly. This assembly is not just a conglomeration of individuals but is the holy people of God, baptised into Christ, united by the Holy Spirit.

For this reason the liturgy is often called the 'work of the people' – a description that also owes its origin to the Greek roots of the word (*laos* and *ergon*). At a more fundamental level still, the liturgy is the work of God among us. It is first and foremost God's loving initiative towards us, God's self-revelation. Only if this has taken place can it also become our response. So all our meetings, all our plans, all our lists and all our books are only the preparation for the event itself, which is the free work of the Holy Spirit among us.

Saint Benedict knew something of this when he referred to the daily offices of his monks as the 'work of God' and came up with the idea of beginning each liturgical office with the invocation 'O God, come to my aid'. We cannot worship unless God is at work in us. Nobody can call Jesus 'Lord' except through the influence of the Holy Spirit. And the Spirit blows, like the wind, whenever and wherever.

Other Sources You Might Find Useful

A Welcome For Your Child: A Guide to Baptism For Parents, Julie Kavanagh and Maeve Mahon (2008)

Bringing Communion to the Sick: A Handbook for Ministers of Holy Communion (2012)

Celebrating the Mass Throughout the Year, National Centre For Liturgy (2011)

Celebrating the Mystery of Faith: A Guide to the Mass, National Centre For Liturgy (2011)

Dying You Destroyed Our Death: Prayers and Reflections to Comfort Those Who Mourn, Andrew G. McGrady, ed. (reprint 2014)

Eucharistic Prayers for Concelebration, International Commission on English in the Liturgy (2011)

Eucharistic Prayers for Masses with Children, Irish Catholic Bishops Conference (2013)

Glenstal Sunday Missal (2012)

Holy Week and Easter Missal (2014)

O Sacred Banquet: Revitalising the Sunday Celebration of the Eucharist (2011)

Our Family Mass (Years A-C) (2012)

Prayer of the Faithful (2013)

Rite of Christian Initiation of Adults, International Commission on English in the Liturgy (reprint 2004)

Sing the Mass (Accompaniment Edition, People Edition and CD), National Centre For Liturgy (2011)

The Funeral Mass (2011)

The Veritas Book of Blessings for All Occasions (2013)

The Wedding Mass (2011)

All publications by Veritas and available at www.veritas.ie and in Veritas shops